SACRAMENTO PUBLIC LIBRARY

D0578841

Supply and Demand

By Linda Crotta Brennan

Illustrated by Rowan Barnes-Murphy

The Child's World®

Published by The Child's World®
1980 Lookout Drive • Mankato, MN 56003-1705
800-599-READ • www.childsworld.com

Acknowledgments
The Child's World®: Mary Berendes, Publishing Director
The Design Lab: Design and production
Red Line Editorial: Editorial direction

Design elements: Eric Krouse/Dreamstime

Copyright © 2013 by The Child's World®
All rights reserved. No part of this book may be
reproduced or utilized in any form or by any means
without written permission from the publisher.

ISBN 9781614732433
LCCN 2012932821

Printed in the United States of America
Mankato, MN
July 2012
PA02122

About the Author
Linda Crotta Brennan has a master's degree in early childhood education. She has taught elementary school and worked in a library. Now, she is a full-time writer. She enjoys learning new things and writing about them. She lives with her husband and goofy golden retriever in Rhode Island. She has three grown daughters.

About the Illustrator
Rowan Barnes-Murphy has created images and characters for children's and adults' books. His drawings have appeared in magazines and newspapers all over the world. He's even drawn for greeting cards and board games. He lives and works in Dorset, in southwest England, and spends time in rural France, where he works in an ancient farmhouse.

Mia looked up from the sign she was making. "How much should we charge?"

Tomás set down a pitcher of lemonade on their new stand. "Our costs were 10¢ a cup."

"Let's charge 20¢," said Mia.

"Sounds good to me," Tomás replied.

Their lemonade stand was in a park with fields for different sports. It was a busy Saturday. Some basketball players bought lemonade after their game.

Next, Tomás and Mia's friend Jack stopped by. Jack was heading to the skateboard park. Families stopped, too. Some had been sitting in bleachers watching a softball game.

Mr. Smith, the softball coach, came over. Tomás and Mia's pitcher was empty.

"Rats," said Mr. Smith. "Some ice cold lemonade sure would hit the spot."

On Sunday, Tomás made two pitchers of lemonade to sell. Mia's mother drove the kids to the park. Tomás and Mia each carried a pitcher of lemonade. Mia's mom brought the cups and napkins from the car.

"So many people wanted our lemonade yesterday," said Mia. "I think we can charge more for it."

"How about 25¢ a cup?" Tomás suggested.

"You kids are following the law of **supply** and **demand**," Mia's mom said. "When demand for a **product** is high, prices go up."

Business is ruled by supply and demand. Supply is how much sellers have. Demand is how much buyers want.

Sunday was very warm and lots of people were at the park. Tomás and Mia sold all of their lemonade by midmorning. Tomás counted the money in their cash box. "At this rate," he said, "it won't be long before I have enough money for that video game I've been saving to buy."

"We did so well that I think we should increase our price again. Let's charge 35¢ for our lemonade tomorrow," Mia said.

Tomás and Mia had two pitchers of lemonade to sell Monday. They charged 35¢ a cup. At noon, they had sold only half of one pitcher. The day before, they had sold two full pitchers by noon. They didn't understand why there was such a change from the day before.

Jack rolled up on his skateboard. He looked at their sign and counted out the change in his pocket. "Thirty-five cents is too much," he said. "I won't have enough money left to buy a candy bar."

"Lots of people must think the price is too high," Mia said. "No one's buying."

"Maybe people will buy the lemonade if we sell it for less," Mia said. "We can have a sale."

"Good idea," said Tomás. "Let's slash the price to 15¢ a cup."

"That's a good price!" said Jack. He bought a cup, then took off on his skateboard. Later, he came back with two of his skateboard friends. Jack told Mr. Smith about the sale, too. He was at the park with his family. They all came over. By midafternoon, Mia and Tomás's pitchers were empty.

When the price of a product goes up, fewer people will want to buy it. The demand for the product will go down. When the demand is low, sellers will lower prices.

On Wednesday, Mr. Smith stopped by again. "We're having softball practice today. I'm sure there'll be lots of thirsty players who'll want lemonade."

"Thanks for letting us know!" said Tomás. He turned to Mia. "If lots of people want lemonade, we should be able to raise our price. How about charging 30¢?"

"That sounds good to me!" Mia grinned. "Let's go home and make lots of lemonade."

Mia and Tomás made six pitchers of lemonade. Morning sales were good. They sold two pitchers by 10:00 a.m., but then sales started to drop.

"I wonder why no one's buying our lemonade anymore," Mia said as a crowd of kids walked by without stopping.

When the price of a product is low, more people are likely to buy that product. The demand for the product will go up. Sellers will raise the price. When the price of a product is high, sellers will make more of it so they can earn more money. The supply will go up.

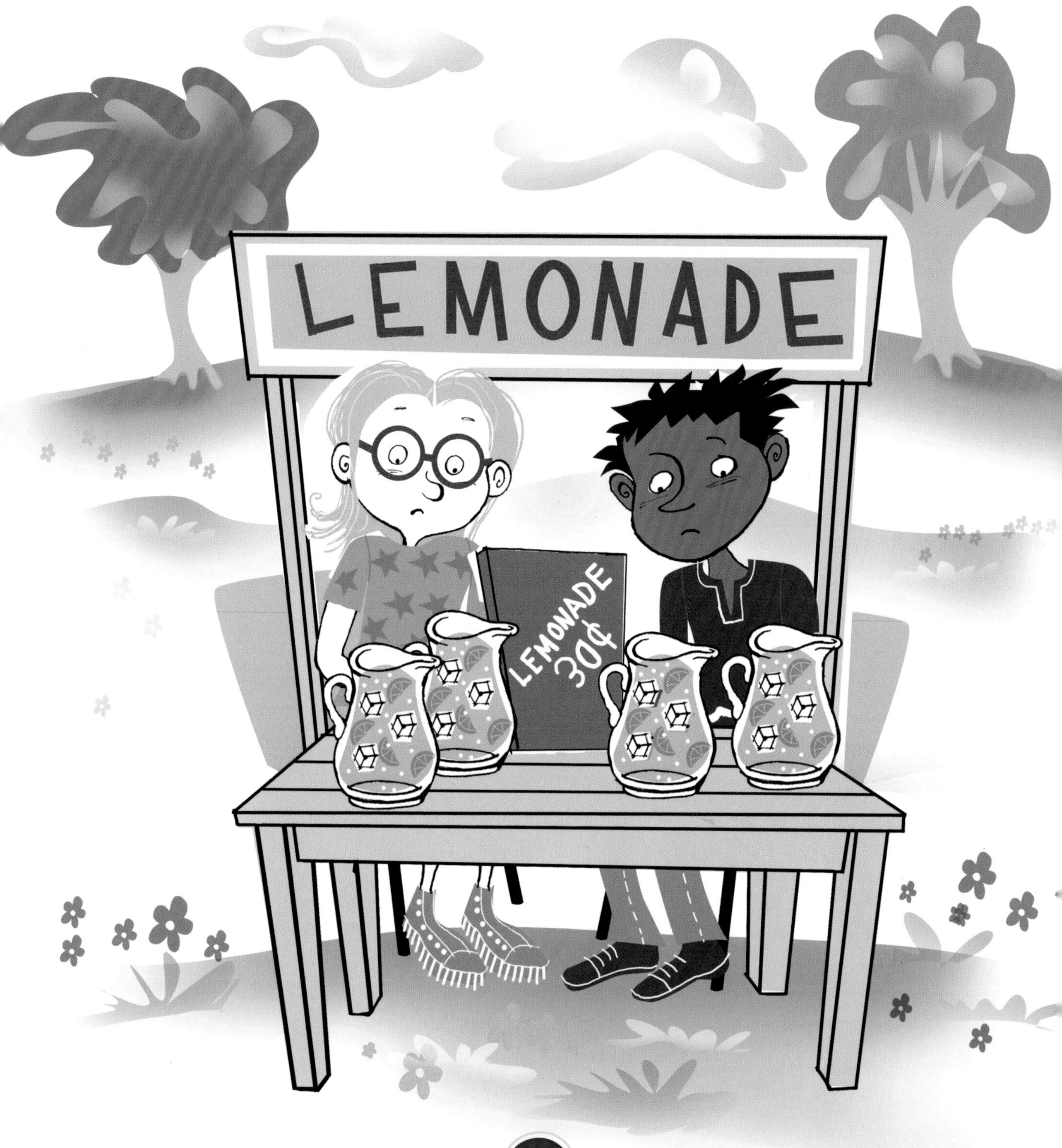
LEMONADE
LEMONADE
30¢

Jack skidded up to the lemonade stand on his bike. "Hi, guys," he said. "Did you see? Someone opened a concession stand on the other side of the park. They're selling soda and hot dogs. The soda costs only 25¢."

Mr. Smith walked by, carrying equipment bags. "It sounds like you have some **competition**."

"We could lower our price to be the same as the soda," said Mia. "But we can't compete with hot dogs."

Tomás scratched his head. "My sister and I made chocolate chip cookies last night. I bet selling cookies with our lemonade would get more customers."

Mr. Smith nodded. "Cookies would give your lemonade product extra value."

Different factors can affect supply and demand. Price is one factor. Other factors include competition and added value.

Tomás ran home and got the cookies. He and Mia sold more lemonade, but not as much as before the concession stand opened.

Jack rode by on his bike. "Hey, I didn't know you were selling cookies, too! I love chocolate chip." He bought two cookies and a cup of lemonade.

"That's it!" said Mia. "We need to **advertise** our product."

Mia posted signs all over the park. Soon, business was booming.

Mr. Smith passed again. Practice was over. He was taking equipment to his car. "Hi, kids. It looks like you've reached **equilibrium**," he said.

"What does that mean?" asked Tomás.

Advertising can increase demand for a product.

"You've priced your product just right. The demand for your lemonade at the price you're charging is just what it should be for the amount of lemonade you have and the price you want to sell at," explained Mr. Smith.

"So, the supply and demand are balanced." said Mia.

"Yes," said Mr. Smith.

"The balance can change, though, right?" Tomás asked. "Like on a rainy day, there wouldn't be much demand for lemonade."

"Sure, lots of things can affect balance," said Mr. Smith. "Even a frost in Florida."

Mia crinkled her brow. "Oh, I know," she said. "If the frost hurt lemon trees, we wouldn't have enough lemons to make our lemonade."

"That means the price of lemons would go up," said Tomás. "And they'd cost more than we would probably want to spend."

Mr. Smith nodded. "Wise business owners study the market."

Mia grinned. "No matter what happens, now we know how to make our business a success."

Tomás grinned, too. "Three cheers for supply and demand!"

Glossary

added value (ad-id VAL-yoo): This is something added to a product to make it worth more. Homemade cookies gave added value to the lemonade.

advertise (AD-vur-tize): To advertise is to share information about a product or service in order to sell it. Mia posted signs in the park to advertise the lemonade stand.

competition (kahm-puh-TISH-uhn): Two or more people or businesses trying to win the same customers is competition. The hot dog stand was in competition with the lemonade stand.

demand (di-MAND): Demand is how much a product or service is wanted. Because the weather was hot and sunny, the demand for lemonade was high.

equilibrium (ee-kwuh-LIB-ree-uhm): To be balanced is to have equilibrium. The demand for lemonade was in equilibrium with the supply of lemonade.

product (PRAH-duhkt): A product is an item that is for sale. Lemonade is the product sold at the lemonade stand.

supply (suh-PLYE): The amount of something available for sale or use is supply. Mia and Tomás have a large supply of lemonade for their stand.

Books

Seidman, David. *The Young Zillionaire's Guide to Supply and Demand*, New York: Rosen, 2000.

Thompson, Gare. *What Is Supply and Demand?* New York: Crabtree, 2009.

Web Sites

Visit our Web site for links about supply and demand:
childsworld.com/links

Note to Parents, Teachers, and Librarians: We routinely verify our Web links to make sure they are safe and active sites. So encourage your readers to check them out!

Index